TWO-STEP PROBLEMS FOR 2ND GRADERS

Math Books for Kids
Children's Math Books

Speedy Publishing LLC

40 E. Main St. #1156

Newark, DE 19711

www.speedypublishing.com

Copyright 2017

Solve each
two-step problem.
Write the solution in
the space provided.

EXERCISE NO. 1

Solve each equation.
Write the solution in the space provided.

(1) $8 - 4 + 10 \ =$

(2) $10 - 7 + 10 \ =$

(3) $8 + 5 + 5 \ =$

(4) $8 - 4 - 2 \ =$

(5) $10 + 8 - 6 \ =$

(6) $6 + 9 + 9 \ =$

(7) $9 - 5 - 3 \ =$

(8) $5 - 4 + 2 \ =$

(9) $6 - 3 + 8 \ =$

(10) $7 - 2 - 2 \ =$

EXERCISE NO. 2

Solve each equation.
Write the solution in the space provided.

(1) $10 - 9 + 3 \ =$

(2) $9 + 2 + 5 \ =$

(3) $9 - 6 + 7 \ =$

(4) $9 + 2 - 8 \ =$

(5) $5 - 3 + 10 \ =$

(6) $6 + 5 - 6 \ =$

(7) $7 + 8 + 5 \ =$

(8) $6 - 2 + 9 \ =$

(9) $5 + 9 + 10 \ =$

(10) $9 - 2 + 9 \ =$

EXERCISE NO. 3

Solve each equation.
Write the solution in the space provided.

(1) $9 - 4 - 3 \ =$

(2) $5 - 3 + 6 \ =$

(3) $3 + 6 + 4 \ =$

(4) $9 - 4 + 10 \ =$

(5) $10 - 8 + 9 \ =$

(6) $2 + 10 - 4 \ =$

(7) $10 - 5 + 8 \ =$

(8) $9 - 6 + 6 \ =$

(9) $5 + 3 + 5 \ =$

(10) $5 - 2 + 8 \ =$

EXERCISE NO. 4

Solve each equation.
Write the solution in the space provided.

(1) $8 + 8 - 8 =$

(2) $9 - 4 + 5 =$

(3) $8 - 2 + 8 =$

(4) $9 - 8 + 8 =$

(5) $5 + 7 - 2 =$

(6) $7 - 6 + 2 =$

(7) $3 + 9 + 4 =$

(8) $10 - 3 - 4 =$

(9) $6 - 4 + 5 =$

(10) $4 + 6 + 10 =$

EXERCISE NO. 5

Solve each equation.
Write the solution in the space provided.

(1) $6 + 3 - 2 \ =$

(2) $9 - 5 + 10 \ =$

(3) $10 + 4 - 7 \ =$

(4) $7 - 3 + 4 \ =$

(5) $9 - 2 + 9 \ =$

(6) $2 + 7 - 4 \ =$

(7) $10 - 4 + 2 \ =$

(8) $4 - 2 + 7 \ =$

(9) $4 + 9 - 4 \ =$

(10) $3 + 7 - 2 \ =$

EXERCISE NO. 6

Solve each equation.
Write the solution in the space provided.

(1) $7 - 4 + 7 \ =$

(2) $9 + 4 + 10 \ =$

(3) $9 + 4 - 8 \ =$

(4) $8 + 3 - 6 \ =$

(5) $3 - 2 + 2 \ =$

(6) $8 - 6 + 10 \ =$

(7) $10 + 6 - 4 \ =$

(8) $10 - 9 + 2 \ =$

(9) $8 - 4 + 7 \ =$

(10) $10 + 6 + 7 \ =$

EXERCISE NO. 7

Solve each equation.
Write the solution in the space provided.

(1) $9 - 2 - 5 \ =$

(2) $5 + 5 + 2 \ =$

(3) $9 + 9 - 6 \ =$

(4) $10 + 4 - 5 \ =$

(5) $7 + 3 + 5 \ =$

(6) $2 + 10 - 10 \ =$

(7) $6 - 3 + 10 \ =$

(8) $8 - 3 - 4 \ =$

(9) $3 + 6 - 5 \ =$

(10) $4 - 2 + 3 \ =$

EXERCISE NO. 8

Solve each equation.
Write the solution in the space provided.

(1) $9 + 8 + 9 \ =$

(2) $5 + 9 - 3 \ =$

(3) $6 - 4 + 2 \ =$

(4) $5 - 2 + 10 \ =$

(5) $4 + 6 - 4 \ =$

(6) $6 + 5 + 10 \ =$

(7) $8 + 2 - 4 \ =$

(8) $8 - 4 + 2 \ =$

(9) $7 + 7 - 2 \ =$

(10) $5 + 9 + 8 \ =$

EXERCISE NO. 9

Solve each equation.
Write the solution in the space provided.

(1) $5 + 10 + 7 \ =$

(2) $2 + 6 + 4 \ =$

(3) $3 + 3 + 6 \ =$

(4) $6 + 4 - 6 \ =$

(5) $8 + 6 - 3 \ =$

(6) $8 - 7 + 7 \ =$

(7) $8 + 7 + 6 \ =$

(8) $8 + 7 - 6 \ =$

(9) $3 + 3 - 5 \ =$

(10) $4 + 5 + 5 \ =$

EXERCISE NO. 10

Solve each equation.
Write the solution in the space provided.

(1) $6 + 3 - 5 =$

(2) $3 + 2 + 6 =$

(3) $10 - 4 + 4 =$

(4) $5 + 6 + 7 =$

(5) $5 + 6 - 7 =$

(6) $2 + 4 - 4 =$

(7) $10 + 7 + 3 =$

(8) $9 + 9 - 9 =$

(9) $10 - 4 + 10 =$

(10) $7 + 8 + 9 =$

EXERCISE NO. 11

Solve each equation.
Write the solution in the space provided.

(1) $7 \times 4 + 10 =$

(2) $5 \times 10 + 8 =$

(3) $2 \times 9 + 8 =$

(4) $5 \times 10 - 7 =$

(5) $7 \times 4 - 10 =$

(6) $6 \times 8 - 5 =$

(7) $10 \times 5 + 8 =$

(8) $10 \times 5 - 8 =$

(9) $2 \times 9 - 6 =$

(10) $3 \times 2 + 2 =$

EXERCISE NO. 12

Solve each equation.
Write the solution in the space provided.

(1) $9 \times 8 + 4 =$

(2) $9 \times 6 + 9 =$

(3) $6 \times 9 - 8 =$

(4) $2 \times 5 + 3 =$

(5) $10 \times 7 + 8 =$

(6) $9 \times 8 - 9 =$

(7) $10 \times 7 - 2 =$

(8) $5 \times 10 + 7 =$

(9) $8 \times 6 + 2 =$

(10) $4 \times 3 - 5 =$

EXERCISE NO. 13

Solve each equation.
Write the solution in the space provided.

(1) $9 \times 4 - 6 =$

(2) $7 \times 8 - 9 =$

(3) $8 \times 5 + 4 =$

(4) $10 \times 7 + 9 =$

(5) $10 \times 7 - 2 =$

(6) $6 \times 9 - 10 =$

(7) $4 \times 6 - 2 =$

(8) $3 \times 3 - 3 =$

(9) $7 \times 8 + 7 =$

(10) $4 \times 6 + 2 =$

EXERCISE NO. 14

Solve each equation.

Write the solution in the space provided.

(1) $3 \times 7 + 6 =$

(2) $4 \times 9 + 4 =$

(3) $6 \times 4 - 10 =$

(4) $2 \times 3 + 2 =$

(5) $10 \times 2 - 9 =$

(6) $7 \times 6 - 7 =$

(7) $8 \times 5 + 7 =$

(8) $4 \times 9 - 9 =$

(9) $6 \times 8 - 8 =$

(10) $7 \times 6 + 3 =$

EXERCISE NO. 15

Solve each equation.
Write the solution in the space provided.

(1) $9 \times 5 - 9 =$

(2) $2 \times 3 - 5 =$

(3) $3 \times 4 - 9 =$

(4) $7 \times 2 - 7 =$

(5) $3 \times 4 + 6 =$

(6) $4 \times 9 - 2 =$

(7) $10 \times 5 + 10 =$

(8) $5 \times 8 - 6 =$

(9) $10 \times 5 - 2 =$

(10) $4 \times 9 + 4 =$

EXERCISE NO. 16

Solve each equation.
Write the solution in the space provided.

(1) $5 \times 5 + 4 \ =$

(2) $9 \times 3 + 8 \ =$

(3) $6 \times 8 + 3 \ =$

(4) $8 \times 4 + 4 \ =$

(5) $3 \times 9 + 6 \ =$

(6) $3 \times 9 - 9 \ =$

(7) $7 \times 6 + 9 \ =$

(8) $5 \times 7 + 3 \ =$

(9) $4 \times 10 + 3 \ =$

(10) $10 \times 2 + 3 \ =$

EXERCISE NO. 17

Solve each equation.
Write the solution in the space provided.

(1) $\quad 7 \times 2 - 9 \ =$

(2) $\quad 5 \times 3 - 4 \ =$

(3) $\quad 6 \times 10 + 8 \ =$

(4) $\quad 3 \times 5 - 10 \ =$

(5) $\quad 5 \times 10 + 8 \ =$

(6) $\quad 2 \times 4 + 5 \ =$

(7) $\quad 5 \times 3 + 6 \ =$

(8) $\quad 6 \times 10 - 7 \ =$

(9) $\quad 3 \times 5 + 10 \ =$

(10) $\quad 4 \times 6 + 5 \ =$

EXERCISE NO. 18

Solve each equation.
Write the solution in the space provided.

(1) $3 \times 10 - 3 \ =$

(2) $6 \times 4 + 7 \ =$

(3) $9 \times 6 - 10 \ =$

(4) $7 \times 2 + 5 \ =$

(5) $5 \times 3 - 5 \ =$

(6) $4 \times 5 + 2 \ =$

(7) $10 \times 9 - 6 \ =$

(8) $2 \times 8 + 8 \ =$

(9) $4 \times 5 - 7 \ =$

(10) $5 \times 5 + 10 \ =$

EXERCISE NO. 19

Solve each equation.
Write the solution in the space provided.

(1) $6 \times 8 - 7 =$

(2) $6 \times 8 + 5 =$

(3) $10 \times 7 - 3 =$

(4) $4 \times 3 + 4 =$

(5) $7 \times 9 + 2 =$

(6) $3 \times 10 + 6 =$

(7) $9 \times 4 + 5 =$

(8) $5 \times 5 + 3 =$

(9) $10 \times 7 + 7 =$

(10) $4 \times 3 - 6 =$

EXERCISE NO. 20

Solve each equation.
Write the solution in the space provided.

(1) $6 \times 3 - 2 =$

(2) $10 \times 10 + 8 =$

(3) $9 \times 2 + 9 =$

(4) $4 \times 2 + 10 =$

(5) $8 \times 4 - 7 =$

(6) $6 \times 3 + 3 =$

(7) $7 \times 5 + 6 =$

(8) $5 \times 7 - 4 =$

(9) $9 \times 2 - 7 =$

(10) $3 \times 8 - 3 =$

EXERCISE NO. 21

Solve each equation.
Write the solution in the space provided.

(1) $9 \times 4 - 8 =$

(2) $8 \times 5 - 8 =$

(3) $10 \times 2 - 7 =$

(4) $3 \times 6 - 10 =$

(5) $9 \times 4 + 8 =$

(6) $5 \times 8 - 10 =$

(7) $4 \times 7 - 7 =$

(8) $7 \times 10 - 6 =$

(9) $8 \times 5 + 7 =$

(10) $10 \times 2 + 4 =$

EXERCISE NO. 22

Solve each equation.
Write the solution in the space provided.

(1) $6 \times 10 - 9 =$

(2) $6 \times 10 + 5 =$

(3) $3 \times 2 + 10 =$

(4) $10 \times 7 - 4 =$

(5) $8 \times 4 - 2 =$

(6) $9 \times 6 + 9 =$

(7) $2 \times 9 - 3 =$

(8) $7 \times 8 + 7 =$

(9) $7 \times 8 - 7 =$

(10) $9 \times 6 - 2 =$

EXERCISE NO. 23

Solve each equation.
Write the solution in the space provided.

(1) $6 \times 5 + 10 =$

(2) $10 \times 10 + 2 =$

(3) $8 \times 2 - 5 =$

(4) $4 \times 4 + 4 =$

(5) $7 \times 9 + 9 =$

(6) $10 \times 10 - 6 =$

(7) $8 \times 2 + 5 =$

(8) $7 \times 5 + 8 =$

(9) $4 \times 4 - 3 =$

(10) $9 \times 6 + 6 =$

EXERCISE NO. 24

Solve each equation.
Write the solution in the space provided.

(1) $3 \times 8 - 10 =$

(2) $3 \times 8 + 2 =$

(3) $10 \times 5 + 2 =$

(4) $8 \times 2 + 9 =$

(5) $9 \times 10 + 3 =$

(6) $7 \times 7 + 2 =$

(7) $2 \times 9 + 5 =$

(8) $4 \times 4 + 5 =$

(9) $5 \times 3 + 5 =$

(10) $6 \times 6 + 2 =$

EXERCISE NO. 25

Solve each equation.
Write the solution in the space provided.

(1) $5 \times 9 + 2 \ =$

(2) $2 \times 2 + 7 \ =$

(3) $9 \times 6 - 10 \ =$

(4) $7 \times 3 - 7 \ =$

(5) $6 \times 10 + 7 \ =$

(6) $3 \times 8 + 3 \ =$

(7) $5 \times 9 - 9 \ =$

(8) $9 \times 6 + 4 \ =$

(9) $10 \times 4 - 4 \ =$

(10) $6 \times 10 - 5 \ =$

EXERCISE NO. 26

Solve each equation.
Write the solution in the space provided.

(1) $7 \times 6 - 4 =$

(2) $2 \times 2 + 6 =$

(3) $10 \times 7 + 10 =$

(4) $5 \times 5 - 9 =$

(5) $9 \times 4 + 9 =$

(6) $6 \times 9 + 9 =$

(7) $3 \times 8 + 5 =$

(8) $7 \times 6 + 2 =$

(9) $10 \times 7 - 6 =$

(10) $9 \times 4 - 7 =$

EXERCISE NO. 27

Solve each equation.
Write the solution in the space provided.

(1) $2 \times 6 + 4 =$

(2) $3 \times 9 + 4 =$

(3) $9 \times 8 - 7 =$

(4) $6 \times 2 + 5 =$

(5) $6 \times 2 - 9 =$

(6) $10 \times 3 + 7 =$

(7) $3 \times 9 - 9 =$

(8) $8 \times 4 + 8 =$

(9) $9 \times 8 + 4 =$

(10) $5 \times 10 + 2 =$

EXERCISE NO. 28

Solve each equation.
Write the solution in the space provided.

(1) $8 \times 10 + 6 \ =$

(2) $10 \times 7 - 5 \ =$

(3) $10 \times 7 + 3 \ =$

(4) $5 \times 6 + 2 \ =$

(5) $3 \times 3 - 3 \ =$

(6) $9 \times 9 - 3 \ =$

(7) $8 \times 10 - 3 \ =$

(8) $5 \times 2 - 8 \ =$

(9) $5 \times 2 + 5 \ =$

(10) $5 \times 6 - 3 \ =$

EXERCISE NO. 29

Solve each equation.
Write the solution in the space provided.

(1) $2 \times 8 + 10 \ =$

(2) $4 \times 7 + 4 \ =$

(3) $8 \times 2 - 9 \ =$

(4) $7 \times 5 - 6 \ =$

(5) $6 \times 10 + 4 \ =$

(6) $3 \times 4 - 2 \ =$

(7) $6 \times 3 - 6 \ =$

(8) $7 \times 5 + 3 \ =$

(9) $2 \times 8 - 4 \ =$

(10) $9 \times 6 - 2 \ =$

EXERCISE NO. 30

Solve each equation.
Write the solution in the space provided.

(1) $5 \times 8 + 5 =$

(2) $3 \times 6 + 5 =$

(3) $5 \times 8 - 9 =$

(4) $10 \times 9 - 2 =$

(5) $2 \times 7 + 7 =$

(6) $9 \times 10 + 3 =$

(7) $6 \times 4 - 5 =$

(8) $9 \times 10 - 2 =$

(9) $3 \times 6 - 3 =$

(10) $2 \times 7 - 2 =$

EXERCISE NO. 31

Solve each equation.
Write the solution in the space provided.

(1) $6 \times 10 + 6 \ =$

(2) $9 \times 7 - 8 \ =$

(3) $4 \times 9 - 7 \ =$

(4) $6 \times 10 - 4 \ =$

(5) $4 \times 5 + 10 \ =$

(6) $4 \times 9 + 6 \ =$

(7) $2 \times 6 - 10 \ =$

(8) $8 \times 4 + 8 \ =$

(9) $5 \times 8 - 9 \ =$

(10) $5 \times 8 + 2 \ =$

EXERCISE NO. 32

Solve each equation.
Write the solution in the space provided.

(1) $9 \times 4 + 10 \ =$

(2) $4 \times 2 - 3 \ =$

(3) $7 \times 6 + 9 \ =$

(4) $9 \times 4 - 3 \ =$

(5) $6 \times 7 + 8 \ =$

(6) $5 \times 9 - 9 \ =$

(7) $7 \times 6 - 10 \ =$

(8) $8 \times 10 - 2 \ =$

(9) $3 \times 5 - 8 \ =$

(10) $2 \times 8 - 5 \ =$

EXERCISE NO. 33

Solve each equation.
Write the solution in the space provided.

(1) $8 \times 9 - 8 =$

(2) $7 \times 10 - 9 =$

(3) $3 \times 7 + 8 =$

(4) $7 \times 10 + 7 =$

(5) $7 \times 8 + 4 =$

(6) $6 \times 6 - 8 =$

(7) $7 \times 8 - 8 =$

(8) $6 \times 6 + 5 =$

(9) $9 \times 4 + 8 =$

(10) $3 \times 7 - 3 =$

EXERCISE NO. 34

Solve each equation.
Write the solution in the space provided.

(1) $9 \times 5 + 7 =$

(2) $5 \times 7 + 6 =$

(3) $6 \times 4 + 4 =$

(4) $3 \times 10 + 5 =$

(5) $3 \times 10 - 3 =$

(6) $5 \times 7 - 2 =$

(7) $10 \times 9 - 4 =$

(8) $8 \times 2 - 3 =$

(9) $3 \times 8 - 2 =$

(10) $7 \times 10 + 8 =$

EXERCISE NO. 35

Solve each equation.
Write the solution in the space provided.

(1) $10 \times 8 + 3 \ =$

(2) $8 \times 9 + 3 \ =$

(3) $4 \times 6 + 9 \ =$

(4) $5 \times 6 + 6 \ =$

(5) $8 \times 9 - 5 \ =$

(6) $4 \times 5 + 6 \ =$

(7) $10 \times 8 - 10 \ =$

(8) $9 \times 3 - 8 \ =$

(9) $4 \times 5 - 5 \ =$

(10) $7 \times 10 + 2 \ =$

EXERCISE NO. 36

Solve each equation.
Write the solution in the space provided.

(1) $10 \times 7 + 9 \ =$

(2) $4 \times 5 + 8 \ =$

(3) $3 \times 6 - 8 \ =$

(4) $6 \times 9 - 5 \ =$

(5) $9 \times 10 - 9 \ =$

(6) $6 \times 9 + 5 \ =$

(7) $5 \times 8 + 10 \ =$

(8) $8 \times 4 + 8 \ =$

(9) $8 \times 4 - 7 \ =$

(10) $2 \times 3 - 3 \ =$

EXERCISE NO. 37

Solve each equation.
Write the solution in the space provided.

(1) $3 \times 10 - 6 =$

(2) $3 \times 10 + 10 =$

(3) $9 \times 6 + 10 =$

(4) $3 \times 8 - 10 =$

(5) $7 \times 9 + 6 =$

(6) $5 \times 3 + 8 =$

(7) $6 \times 7 - 2 =$

(8) $8 \times 4 + 4 =$

(9) $6 \times 7 + 5 =$

(10) $10 \times 5 + 10 =$

EXERCISE NO. 38

Solve each equation.
Write the solution in the space provided.

(1) $5 \times 7 + 2 =$

(2) $3 \times 9 - 7 =$

(3) $9 \times 8 - 8 =$

(4) $4 \times 5 - 8 =$

(5) $6 \times 6 + 4 =$

(6) $7 \times 10 + 4 =$

(7) $3 \times 9 + 3 =$

(8) $7 \times 9 - 8 =$

(9) $7 \times 9 + 3 =$

(10) $5 \times 7 - 6 =$

EXERCISE NO. 39

Solve each equation.
Write the solution in the space provided.

(1) $3 \times 10 - 5 \ =$

(6) $4 \times 4 + 4 \ =$

(2) $7 \times 6 + 4 \ =$

(7) $9 \times 3 - 5 \ =$

(3) $2 \times 7 - 6 \ =$

(8) $2 \times 7 + 10 \ =$

(4) $8 \times 5 + 8 \ =$

(9) $8 \times 5 - 9 \ =$

(5) $5 \times 2 + 6 \ =$

(10) $6 \times 9 + 9 \ =$

EXERCISE NO. 40

Solve each equation.
Write the solution in the space provided.

(1) $4 \times 10 + 3 \ =$

(2) $8 \times 9 + 10 \ =$

(3) $6 \times 3 + 8 \ =$

(4) $2 \times 5 - 9 \ =$

(5) $10 \times 2 + 9 \ =$

(6) $7 \times 4 - 6 \ =$

(7) $9 \times 8 + 5 \ =$

(8) $5 \times 7 - 8 \ =$

(9) $5 \times 7 + 3 \ =$

(10) $9 \times 8 - 2 \ =$

EXERCISE NO. 41

Solve each equation.
Write the solution in the space provided.

(1) $6 \times 10 + 2 =$

(2) $6 \times 3 - 7 =$

(3) $5 \times 6 - 5 =$

(4) $4 \times 4 + 7 =$

(5) $6 \times 10 - 6 =$

(6) $7 \times 9 - 8 =$

(7) $4 \times 4 - 6 =$

(8) $2 \times 8 + 3 =$

(9) $7 \times 9 + 3 =$

(10) $5 \times 6 + 8 =$

EXERCISE NO. 42

Solve each equation.
Write the solution in the space provided.

(1) $9 \times 2 - 6 \ =$

(2) $5 \times 5 - 6 \ =$

(3) $6 \times 7 - 10 \ =$

(4) $2 \times 3 + 9 \ =$

(5) $4 \times 9 + 3 \ =$

(6) $6 \times 7 + 9 \ =$

(7) $6 \times 6 + 4 \ =$

(8) $4 \times 9 - 6 \ =$

(9) $5 \times 5 + 3 \ =$

(10) $3 \times 10 - 3 \ =$

EXERCISE NO. 43

Solve each equation.
Write the solution in the space provided.

(1) $4 \times 5 + 4 \ =$

(2) $6 \times 9 + 2 \ =$

(3) $9 \times 4 + 5 \ =$

(4) $5 \times 9 + 3 \ =$

(5) $3 \times 8 + 5 \ =$

(6) $5 \times 10 - 4 \ =$

(7) $7 \times 2 - 3 \ =$

(8) $5 \times 10 + 4 \ =$

(9) $10 \times 7 - 4 \ =$

(10) $9 \times 4 - 5 \ =$

EXERCISE NO. 44

Solve each equation.
Write the solution in the space provided.

(1) $3 \times 7 + 2 =$

(2) $3 \times 7 - 8 =$

(3) $9 \times 3 - 6 =$

(4) $8 \times 6 - 9 =$

(5) $9 \times 3 + 6 =$

(6) $2 \times 5 + 10 =$

(7) $10 \times 8 - 7 =$

(8) $2 \times 5 - 6 =$

(9) $4 \times 9 + 3 =$

(10) $4 \times 9 - 8 =$

EXERCISE NO. 45

Solve each equation.
Write the solution in the space provided.

(1) $2 \times 8 + 5 =$

(2) $9 \times 5 - 9 =$

(3) $9 \times 6 + 3 =$

(4) $6 \times 7 + 7 =$

(5) $8 \times 9 + 4 =$

(6) $4 \times 10 + 6 =$

(7) $9 \times 5 + 2 =$

(8) $9 \times 6 - 7 =$

(9) $5 \times 3 + 6 =$

(10) $10 \times 2 - 4 =$

EXERCISE NO. 46

Solve each equation.
Write the solution in the space provided.

(1) $2 \times 9 - 8 =$

(2) $7 \times 5 + 2 =$

(3) $6 \times 7 - 6 =$

(4) $10 \times 8 + 6 =$

(5) $4 \times 6 + 3 =$

(6) $3 \times 2 + 3 =$

(7) $2 \times 9 + 7 =$

(8) $4 \times 6 - 10 =$

(9) $5 \times 3 + 9 =$

(10) $10 \times 8 - 5 =$

EXERCISE NO. 1

(1) $8 - 4 + 10 = 14$

(2) $10 - 7 + 10 = 13$

(3) $8 + 5 + 5 = 18$

(4) $8 - 4 - 2 = 2$

(5) $10 + 8 - 6 = 12$

(6) $6 + 9 + 9 = 24$

(7) $9 - 5 - 3 = 1$

(8) $5 - 4 + 2 = 3$

(9) $6 - 3 + 8 = 11$

(10) $7 - 2 - 2 = 3$

EXERCISE NO. 2

(1) $10 - 9 + 3 = 4$

(2) $9 + 2 + 5 = 16$

(3) $9 - 6 + 7 = 10$

(4) $9 + 2 - 8 = 3$

(5) $5 - 3 + 10 = 12$

(6) $6 + 5 - 6 = 5$

(7) $7 + 8 + 5 = 20$

(8) $6 - 2 + 9 = 13$

(9) $5 + 9 + 10 = 24$

(10) $9 - 2 + 9 = 16$

EXERCISE NO. 3

(1) $9 - 4 - 3 = 2$
(2) $5 - 3 + 6 = 8$
(3) $3 + 6 + 4 = 13$
(4) $9 - 4 + 10 = 15$
(5) $10 - 8 + 9 = 11$
(6) $2 + 10 - 4 = 8$
(7) $10 - 5 + 8 = 13$
(8) $9 - 6 + 6 = 9$
(9) $5 + 3 + 5 = 13$
(10) $5 - 2 + 8 = 11$

EXERCISE NO. 4

(1) $8 + 8 - 8 = 8$
(2) $9 - 4 + 5 = 10$
(3) $8 - 2 + 8 = 14$
(4) $9 - 8 + 8 = 9$
(5) $5 + 7 - 2 = 10$
(6) $7 - 6 + 2 = 3$
(7) $3 + 9 + 4 = 16$
(8) $10 - 3 - 4 = 3$
(9) $6 - 4 + 5 = 7$
(10) $4 + 6 + 10 = 20$

EXERCISE NO. 5

(1) $6 + 3 - 2 = 7$
(2) $9 - 5 + 10 = 14$
(3) $10 + 4 - 7 = 7$
(4) $7 - 3 + 4 = 8$
(5) $9 - 2 + 9 = 16$
(6) $2 + 7 - 4 = 5$
(7) $10 - 4 + 2 = 8$
(8) $4 - 2 + 7 = 9$
(9) $4 + 9 - 4 = 9$
(10) $3 + 7 - 2 = 8$

EXERCISE NO. 6

(1) $7 - 4 + 7 = 10$
(2) $9 + 4 + 10 = 23$
(3) $9 + 4 - 8 = 5$
(4) $8 + 3 - 6 = 5$
(5) $3 - 2 + 2 = 3$
(6) $8 - 6 + 10 = 12$
(7) $10 + 6 - 4 = 12$
(8) $10 - 9 + 2 = 3$
(9) $8 - 4 + 7 = 11$
(10) $10 + 6 + 7 = 23$

EXERCISE NO. 7

(1)	$9 - 2 - 5 = 2$
(2)	$5 + 5 + 2 = 12$
(3)	$9 + 9 - 6 = 12$
(4)	$10 + 4 - 5 = 9$
(5)	$7 + 3 + 5 = 15$
(6)	$2 + 10 - 10 = 2$
(7)	$6 - 3 + 10 = 13$
(8)	$8 - 3 - 4 = 1$
(9)	$3 + 6 - 5 = 4$
(10)	$4 - 2 + 3 = 5$

EXERCISE NO. 8

(1)	$9 + 8 + 9 = 26$
(2)	$5 + 9 - 3 = 11$
(3)	$6 - 4 + 2 = 4$
(4)	$5 - 2 + 10 = 13$
(5)	$4 + 6 - 4 = 6$
(6)	$6 + 5 + 10 = 21$
(7)	$8 + 2 - 4 = 6$
(8)	$8 - 4 + 2 = 6$
(9)	$7 + 7 - 2 = 12$
(10)	$5 + 9 + 8 = 22$

EXERCISE NO. 9

(1)	$5 + 10 + 7 = 22$
(2)	$2 + 6 + 4 = 12$
(3)	$3 + 3 + 6 = 12$
(4)	$6 + 4 - 6 = 4$
(5)	$8 + 6 - 3 = 11$
(6)	$8 - 7 + 7 = 8$
(7)	$8 + 7 + 6 = 21$
(8)	$8 + 7 - 6 = 9$
(9)	$3 + 3 - 5 = 1$
(10)	$4 + 5 + 5 = 14$

EXERCISE NO. 10

(1)	$6 + 3 - 5 = 4$
(2)	$3 + 2 + 6 = 11$
(3)	$10 - 4 + 4 = 10$
(4)	$5 + 6 + 7 = 18$
(5)	$5 + 6 - 7 = 4$
(6)	$2 + 4 - 4 = 2$
(7)	$10 + 7 + 3 = 20$
(8)	$9 + 9 - 9 = 9$
(9)	$10 - 4 + 10 = 16$
(10)	$7 + 8 + 9 = 24$

EXERCISE NO. 11

(1) $7 \times 4 + 10 = 38$
(2) $5 \times 10 + 8 = 58$
(3) $2 \times 9 + 8 = 26$
(4) $5 \times 10 - 7 = 43$
(5) $7 \times 4 - 10 = 18$
(6) $6 \times 8 - 5 = 43$
(7) $10 \times 5 + 8 = 58$
(8) $10 \times 5 - 8 = 42$
(9) $2 \times 9 - 6 = 12$
(10) $3 \times 2 + 2 = 8$

EXERCISE NO. 12

(1) $9 \times 8 + 4 = 76$
(2) $9 \times 6 + 9 = 63$
(3) $6 \times 9 - 8 = 46$
(4) $2 \times 5 + 3 = 13$
(5) $10 \times 7 + 8 = 78$
(6) $9 \times 8 - 9 = 63$
(7) $10 \times 7 - 2 = 68$
(8) $5 \times 10 + 7 = 57$
(9) $8 \times 6 + 2 = 50$
(10) $4 \times 3 - 5 = 7$

EXERCISE NO. 13

(1) $9 \times 4 - 6 = 30$
(2) $7 \times 8 - 9 = 47$
(3) $8 \times 5 + 4 = 44$
(4) $10 \times 7 + 9 = 79$
(5) $10 \times 7 - 2 = 68$
(6) $6 \times 9 - 10 = 44$
(7) $4 \times 6 - 2 = 22$
(8) $3 \times 3 - 3 = 6$
(9) $7 \times 8 + 7 = 63$
(10) $4 \times 6 + 2 = 26$

EXERCISE NO. 14

(1) $3 \times 7 + 6 = 27$
(2) $4 \times 9 + 4 = 40$
(3) $6 \times 4 - 10 = 14$
(4) $2 \times 3 + 2 = 8$
(5) $10 \times 2 - 9 = 11$
(6) $7 \times 6 - 7 = 35$
(7) $8 \times 5 + 7 = 47$
(8) $4 \times 9 - 9 = 27$
(9) $6 \times 8 - 8 = 40$
(10) $7 \times 6 + 3 = 45$

EXERCISE NO. 15

(1)	$9 \times 5 - 9$	$=$	36
(2)	$2 \times 3 - 5$	$=$	1
(3)	$3 \times 4 - 9$	$=$	3
(4)	$7 \times 2 - 7$	$=$	7
(5)	$3 \times 4 + 6$	$=$	18
(6)	$4 \times 9 - 2$	$=$	34
(7)	$10 \times 5 + 10$	$=$	60
(8)	$5 \times 8 - 6$	$=$	34
(9)	$10 \times 5 - 2$	$=$	48
(10)	$4 \times 9 + 4$	$=$	40

EXERCISE NO. 16

(1)	$5 \times 5 + 4$	$=$	29
(2)	$9 \times 3 + 8$	$=$	35
(3)	$6 \times 8 + 3$	$=$	51
(4)	$8 \times 4 + 4$	$=$	36
(5)	$3 \times 9 + 6$	$=$	33
(6)	$3 \times 9 - 9$	$=$	18
(7)	$7 \times 6 + 9$	$=$	51
(8)	$5 \times 7 + 3$	$=$	38
(9)	$4 \times 10 + 3$	$=$	43
(10)	$10 \times 2 + 3$	$=$	23

EXERCISE NO. 17

(1)	$7 \times 2 - 9$	$=$	5
(2)	$5 \times 3 - 4$	$=$	11
(3)	$6 \times 10 + 8$	$=$	68
(4)	$3 \times 5 - 10$	$=$	5
(5)	$5 \times 10 + 8$	$=$	58
(6)	$2 \times 4 + 5$	$=$	13
(7)	$5 \times 3 + 6$	$=$	21
(8)	$6 \times 10 - 7$	$=$	53
(9)	$3 \times 5 + 10$	$=$	25
(10)	$4 \times 6 + 5$	$=$	29

EXERCISE NO. 18

(1)	$3 \times 10 - 3$	$=$	27
(2)	$6 \times 4 + 7$	$=$	31
(3)	$9 \times 6 - 10$	$=$	44
(4)	$7 \times 2 + 5$	$=$	19
(5)	$5 \times 3 - 5$	$=$	10
(6)	$4 \times 5 + 2$	$=$	22
(7)	$10 \times 9 - 6$	$=$	84
(8)	$2 \times 8 + 8$	$=$	24
(9)	$4 \times 5 - 7$	$=$	13
(10)	$5 \times 5 + 10$	$=$	35

EXERCISE NO. 19

(1)	$6 \times 8 - 7 = 41$	
(2)	$6 \times 8 + 5 = 53$	
(3)	$10 \times 7 - 3 = 67$	
(4)	$4 \times 3 + 4 = 16$	
(5)	$7 \times 9 + 2 = 65$	
(6)	$3 \times 10 + 6 = 36$	
(7)	$9 \times 4 + 5 = 41$	
(8)	$5 \times 5 + 3 = 28$	
(9)	$10 \times 7 + 7 = 77$	
(10)	$4 \times 3 - 6 = 6$	

EXERCISE NO. 20

(1)	$6 \times 3 - 2 = 16$	
(2)	$10 \times 10 + 8 = 108$	
(3)	$9 \times 2 + 9 = 27$	
(4)	$4 \times 2 + 10 = 18$	
(5)	$8 \times 4 - 7 = 25$	
(6)	$6 \times 3 + 3 = 21$	
(7)	$7 \times 5 + 6 = 41$	
(8)	$5 \times 7 - 4 = 31$	
(9)	$9 \times 2 - 7 = 11$	
(10)	$3 \times 8 - 3 = 21$	

EXERCISE NO. 21

(1)	$9 \times 4 - 8 = 28$	
(2)	$8 \times 5 - 8 = 32$	
(3)	$10 \times 2 - 7 = 13$	
(4)	$3 \times 6 - 10 = 8$	
(5)	$9 \times 4 + 8 = 44$	
(6)	$5 \times 8 - 10 = 30$	
(7)	$4 \times 7 - 7 = 21$	
(8)	$7 \times 10 - 6 = 64$	
(9)	$8 \times 5 + 7 = 47$	
(10)	$10 \times 2 + 4 = 24$	

EXERCISE NO. 22

(1)	$6 \times 10 - 9 = 51$	
(2)	$6 \times 10 + 5 = 65$	
(3)	$3 \times 2 + 10 = 16$	
(4)	$10 \times 7 - 4 = 66$	
(5)	$8 \times 4 - 2 = 30$	
(6)	$9 \times 6 + 9 = 63$	
(7)	$2 \times 9 - 3 = 15$	
(8)	$7 \times 8 + 7 = 63$	
(9)	$7 \times 8 - 7 = 49$	
(10)	$9 \times 6 - 2 = 52$	

(1) $6 \times 5 + 10 = 40$
(2) $10 \times 10 + 2 = 102$
(3) $8 \times 2 - 5 = 11$
(4) $4 \times 4 + 4 = 20$
(5) $7 \times 9 + 9 = 72$
(6) $10 \times 10 - 6 = 94$
(7) $8 \times 2 + 5 = 21$
(8) $7 \times 5 + 8 = 43$
(9) $4 \times 4 - 3 = 13$
(10) $9 \times 6 + 6 = 60$

(1) $3 \times 8 - 10 = 14$
(2) $3 \times 8 + 2 = 26$
(3) $10 \times 5 + 2 = 52$
(4) $8 \times 2 + 9 = 25$
(5) $9 \times 10 + 3 = 93$
(6) $7 \times 7 + 2 = 51$
(7) $2 \times 9 + 5 = 23$
(8) $4 \times 4 + 5 = 21$
(9) $5 \times 3 + 5 = 20$
(10) $6 \times 6 + 2 = 38$

(1) $5 \times 9 + 2 = 47$
(2) $2 \times 2 + 7 = 11$
(3) $9 \times 6 - 10 = 44$
(4) $7 \times 3 - 7 = 14$
(5) $6 \times 10 + 7 = 67$
(6) $3 \times 8 + 3 = 27$
(7) $5 \times 9 - 9 = 36$
(8) $9 \times 6 + 4 = 58$
(9) $10 \times 4 - 4 = 36$
(10) $6 \times 10 - 5 = 55$

(1) $7 \times 6 - 4 = 38$
(2) $2 \times 2 + 6 = 10$
(3) $10 \times 7 + 10 = 80$
(4) $5 \times 5 - 9 = 16$
(5) $9 \times 4 + 9 = 45$
(6) $6 \times 9 + 9 = 63$
(7) $3 \times 8 + 5 = 29$
(8) $7 \times 6 + 2 = 44$
(9) $10 \times 7 - 6 = 64$
(10) $9 \times 4 - 7 = 29$

EXERCISE NO. 27

(1)	$2 \times 6 + 4$	$=$	16
(2)	$3 \times 9 + 4$	$=$	31
(3)	$9 \times 8 - 7$	$=$	65
(4)	$6 \times 2 + 5$	$=$	17
(5)	$6 \times 2 - 9$	$=$	3
(6)	$10 \times 3 + 7$	$=$	37
(7)	$3 \times 9 - 9$	$=$	18
(8)	$8 \times 4 + 8$	$=$	40
(9)	$9 \times 8 + 4$	$=$	76
(10)	$5 \times 10 + 2$	$=$	52

EXERCISE NO. 28

(1)	$8 \times 10 + 6$	$=$	86
(2)	$10 \times 7 - 5$	$=$	65
(3)	$10 \times 7 + 3$	$=$	73
(4)	$5 \times 6 + 2$	$=$	32
(5)	$3 \times 3 - 3$	$=$	6
(6)	$9 \times 9 - 3$	$=$	78
(7)	$8 \times 10 - 3$	$=$	77
(8)	$5 \times 2 - 8$	$=$	2
(9)	$5 \times 2 + 5$	$=$	15
(10)	$5 \times 6 - 3$	$=$	27

EXERCISE NO. 29

(1)	$2 \times 8 + 10$	$=$	26
(2)	$4 \times 7 + 4$	$=$	32
(3)	$8 \times 2 - 9$	$=$	7
(4)	$7 \times 5 - 6$	$=$	29
(5)	$6 \times 10 + 4$	$=$	64
(6)	$3 \times 4 - 2$	$=$	10
(7)	$6 \times 3 - 6$	$=$	12
(8)	$7 \times 5 + 3$	$=$	38
(9)	$2 \times 8 - 4$	$=$	12
(10)	$9 \times 6 - 2$	$=$	52

EXERCISE NO. 30

(1)	$5 \times 8 + 5$	$=$	45
(2)	$3 \times 6 + 5$	$=$	23
(3)	$5 \times 8 - 9$	$=$	31
(4)	$10 \times 9 - 2$	$=$	88
(5)	$2 \times 7 + 7$	$=$	21
(6)	$9 \times 10 + 3$	$=$	93
(7)	$6 \times 4 - 5$	$=$	19
(8)	$9 \times 10 - 2$	$=$	88
(9)	$3 \times 6 - 3$	$=$	15
(10)	$2 \times 7 - 2$	$=$	12

EXERCISE NO. 31

(1) $6 \times 10 + 6 = 66$
(2) $9 \times 7 - 8 = 55$
(3) $4 \times 9 - 7 = 29$
(4) $6 \times 10 - 4 = 56$
(5) $4 \times 5 + 10 = 30$
(6) $4 \times 9 + 6 = 42$
(7) $2 \times 6 - 10 = 2$
(8) $8 \times 4 + 8 = 40$
(9) $5 \times 8 - 9 = 31$
(10) $5 \times 8 + 2 = 42$

EXERCISE NO. 32

(1) $9 \times 4 + 10 = 46$
(2) $4 \times 2 - 3 = 5$
(3) $7 \times 6 + 9 = 51$
(4) $9 \times 4 - 3 = 33$
(5) $6 \times 7 + 8 = 50$
(6) $5 \times 9 - 9 = 36$
(7) $7 \times 6 - 10 = 32$
(8) $8 \times 10 - 2 = 78$
(9) $3 \times 5 - 8 = 7$
(10) $2 \times 8 - 5 = 11$

EXERCISE NO. 33

(1) $8 \times 9 - 8 = 64$
(2) $7 \times 10 - 9 = 61$
(3) $3 \times 7 + 8 = 29$
(4) $7 \times 10 + 7 = 77$
(5) $7 \times 8 + 4 = 60$
(6) $6 \times 6 - 8 = 28$
(7) $7 \times 8 - 8 = 48$
(8) $6 \times 6 + 5 = 41$
(9) $9 \times 4 + 8 = 44$
(10) $3 \times 7 - 3 = 18$

EXERCISE NO. 34

(1) $9 \times 5 + 7 = 52$
(2) $5 \times 7 + 6 = 41$
(3) $6 \times 4 + 4 = 28$
(4) $3 \times 10 + 5 = 35$
(5) $3 \times 10 - 3 = 27$
(6) $5 \times 7 - 2 = 33$
(7) $10 \times 9 - 4 = 86$
(8) $8 \times 2 - 3 = 13$
(9) $3 \times 8 - 2 = 22$
(10) $7 \times 10 + 8 = 78$

EXERCISE NO. 35

(1)	$10 \times 8 + 3$	$=$	83
(2)	$8 \times 9 + 3$	$=$	75
(3)	$4 \times 6 + 9$	$=$	33
(4)	$5 \times 6 + 6$	$=$	36
(5)	$8 \times 9 - 5$	$=$	67
(6)	$4 \times 5 + 6$	$=$	26
(7)	$10 \times 8 - 10$	$=$	70
(8)	$9 \times 3 - 8$	$=$	19
(9)	$4 \times 5 - 5$	$=$	15
(10)	$7 \times 10 + 2$	$=$	72

EXERCISE NO. 36

(1)	$10 \times 7 + 9$	$=$	79
(2)	$4 \times 5 + 8$	$=$	28
(3)	$3 \times 6 - 8$	$=$	10
(4)	$6 \times 9 - 5$	$=$	49
(5)	$9 \times 10 - 9$	$=$	81
(6)	$6 \times 9 + 5$	$=$	59
(7)	$5 \times 8 + 10$	$=$	50
(8)	$8 \times 4 + 8$	$=$	40
(9)	$8 \times 4 - 7$	$=$	25
(10)	$2 \times 3 - 3$	$=$	3

EXERCISE NO. 37

(1)	$3 \times 10 - 6$	$=$	24
(2)	$3 \times 10 + 10$	$=$	40
(3)	$9 \times 6 + 10$	$=$	64
(4)	$3 \times 8 - 10$	$=$	14
(5)	$7 \times 9 + 6$	$=$	69
(6)	$5 \times 3 + 8$	$=$	23
(7)	$6 \times 7 - 2$	$=$	40
(8)	$8 \times 4 + 4$	$=$	36
(9)	$6 \times 7 + 5$	$=$	47
(10)	$10 \times 5 + 10$	$=$	60

EXERCISE NO. 38

(1)	$5 \times 7 + 2$	$=$	37
(2)	$3 \times 9 - 7$	$=$	20
(3)	$9 \times 8 - 8$	$=$	64
(4)	$4 \times 5 - 8$	$=$	12
(5)	$6 \times 6 + 4$	$=$	40
(6)	$7 \times 10 + 4$	$=$	74
(7)	$3 \times 9 + 3$	$=$	30
(8)	$7 \times 9 - 8$	$=$	55
(9)	$7 \times 9 + 3$	$=$	66
(10)	$5 \times 7 - 6$	$=$	29

(1)	$3 \times 10 - 5 = 25$	(6) $4 \times 4 + 4 = 20$
(2)	$7 \times 6 + 4 = 46$	(7) $9 \times 3 - 5 = 22$
(3)	$2 \times 7 - 6 = 8$	(8) $2 \times 7 + 10 = 24$
(4)	$8 \times 5 + 8 = 48$	(9) $8 \times 5 - 9 = 31$
(5)	$5 \times 2 + 6 = 16$	(10) $6 \times 9 + 9 = 63$

(1)	$4 \times 10 + 3 = 43$	(6) $7 \times 4 - 6 = 22$
(2)	$8 \times 9 + 10 = 82$	(7) $9 \times 8 + 5 = 77$
(3)	$6 \times 3 + 8 = 26$	(8) $5 \times 7 - 8 = 27$
(4)	$2 \times 5 - 9 = 1$	(9) $5 \times 7 + 3 = 38$
(5)	$10 \times 2 + 9 = 29$	(10) $9 \times 8 - 2 = 70$

(1)	$6 \times 10 + 2 = 62$	(6) $7 \times 9 - 8 = 55$
(2)	$6 \times 3 - 7 = 11$	(7) $4 \times 4 - 6 = 10$
(3)	$5 \times 6 - 5 = 25$	(8) $2 \times 8 + 3 = 19$
(4)	$4 \times 4 + 7 = 23$	(9) $7 \times 9 + 3 = 66$
(5)	$6 \times 10 - 6 = 54$	(10) $5 \times 6 + 8 = 38$

(1)	$9 \times 2 - 6 = 12$	(6) $6 \times 7 + 9 = 51$
(2)	$5 \times 5 - 6 = 19$	(7) $6 \times 6 + 4 = 40$
(3)	$6 \times 7 - 10 = 32$	(8) $4 \times 9 - 6 = 30$
(4)	$2 \times 3 + 9 = 15$	(9) $5 \times 5 + 3 = 28$
(5)	$4 \times 9 + 3 = 39$	(10) $3 \times 10 - 3 = 27$

EXERCISE NO. 43

(1) $4 \times 5 + 4 = 24$
(2) $6 \times 9 + 2 = 56$
(3) $9 \times 4 + 5 = 41$
(4) $5 \times 9 + 3 = 48$
(5) $3 \times 8 + 5 = 29$
(6) $5 \times 10 - 4 = 46$
(7) $7 \times 2 - 3 = 11$
(8) $5 \times 10 + 4 = 54$
(9) $10 \times 7 - 4 = 66$
(10) $9 \times 4 - 5 = 31$

EXERCISE NO. 44

(1) $3 \times 7 + 2 = 23$
(2) $3 \times 7 - 8 = 13$
(3) $9 \times 3 - 6 = 21$
(4) $8 \times 6 - 9 = 39$
(5) $9 \times 3 + 6 = 33$
(6) $2 \times 5 + 10 = 20$
(7) $10 \times 8 - 7 = 73$
(8) $2 \times 5 - 6 = 4$
(9) $4 \times 9 + 3 = 39$
(10) $4 \times 9 - 8 = 28$

EXERCISE NO. 45

(1) $2 \times 8 + 5 = 21$
(2) $9 \times 5 - 9 = 36$
(3) $9 \times 6 + 3 = 57$
(4) $6 \times 7 + 7 = 49$
(5) $8 \times 9 + 4 = 76$
(6) $4 \times 10 + 6 = 46$
(7) $9 \times 5 + 2 = 47$
(8) $9 \times 6 - 7 = 47$
(9) $5 \times 3 + 6 = 21$
(10) $10 \times 2 - 4 = 16$

EXERCISE NO. 46

(1) $2 \times 9 - 8 = 10$
(2) $7 \times 5 + 2 = 37$
(3) $6 \times 7 - 6 = 36$
(4) $10 \times 8 + 6 = 86$
(5) $4 \times 6 + 3 = 27$
(6) $3 \times 2 + 3 = 9$
(7) $2 \times 9 + 7 = 25$
(8) $4 \times 6 - 10 = 14$
(9) $5 \times 3 + 9 = 24$
(10) $10 \times 8 - 5 = 75$

Visit

BABY PROFESSOR
EDUCATION KIDS

www.BabyProfessorBooks.com
to download Free Baby Professor eBooks
and view our catalog of new and exciting
Children's Books